'**ARRY**

The funniest Harry Redknapp quotes!

by Gordon Law

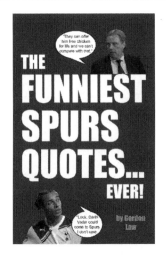 
Copyright © 2017 by Gordon Law

gordonlawauthor@yahoo.com

Printed in Europe and the USA
ISBN-13: 978-1979108263
ISBN-10: 1979108269

Photos courtesy of: Mitch Gunn/Shutterstock.com

Contents

Introduction..4

Talking Balls...7

Media Circus...23

Call the Manager...31

Ref Justice...43

Lifestyle Choice..49

Can You Manage?...67

A Funny Old Game..93

Player Power..113

Scary...127

Introduction

Harry Redknapp stands out as one of English football's true characters. He's also proven himself to be one of the finest club coaches and the best manager that England never had.

Typically friendly with the media, the interviews from his car window on transfer deadline day have become the stuff of legend. He's a cheeky chappy from East London and the master of a comic aside – but don't ever call him a wheeler and dealer.

A Sky TV reporter once suggested he was just that and Harry lost his rag, telling him to "F*ck off... I'm not a f*cking dealer – I'm a f*cking football manager."

The hilarious outburst by the man who has a reputation for building a squad of bargains was a classic. As was the clip where Harry got hit by the ball during a training ground interview and blasted the offending player live on air. Harry has never been afraid to speak his mind but he's probably best known for his wicked sense of humour and telling a great anecdote.

Whether it's lamenting the modern-day player, mixing up his metaphors or getting in trouble with the wife, Harry's quips are comedy gold.

Anything from self-deprecating: "I've got coaching badges but they came out of a Corn Flakes packet." To making light of a heavy defeat: "I've just been given a video recording of the game and I'm going to tape Neighbours over it."

Harry's brutal honesty and witty lines make him one of the game's best personalities and I hope you enjoy this bumper collection of quotes.

Gordon Law

'ARRY – The funniest Harry Redknapp quotes!

TALKING BALLS

"When Rio Ferdinand went in goal, I wasn't too worried. I saw him play in goal when he was a kid and I knew he wasn't very good."

Harry Redknapp had a good feeling when the Manchester United defender took the gloves in Portsmouth's FA Cup win

"Today we didn't capitulate – I think that's the posh word for it."

The Pompey boss swallows a dictionary

"I was going to pull him off at half-time, but he got a piece of orange like everyone else."

Harry on Paolo Di Canio

"I think a lot of players would have kicked him a lot harder."

Harry defends Chelsea star Eden Hazard after he was given a red card for kicking a ballboy

"Joe Cole missed an open goal that my f*cking missus could have scored."

Harry is not happy

"Palacios is suspended – he likes tackling you see – so I don't know if he'll be any good in our team!"

On new Tottenham signing Wilson Palacios

"He said that? He's got to be a masochist. How can anyone in charge of teams like ours say it's fun watching defending like that?"

Harry reacts after his Norwich counterpart Nigel Worthington said Southampton's 4-3 win was: "A terrific game, even on the losing side I could enjoy it."

"I stood there all day with a plastic angel in my pocket. I believe in fate – I'm as silly as a bunch of lights!"

The Saints manager on the lucky mascot given to him by his wife for a relegation six-pointer at Crystal Palace

"Ramon Vega went down like he was dead. I thought he had broken his leg but he only broke a tie-up."
Harry on play acting

"[Loic] Remy looked like he might be getting over that groin strain. He showed a few flashes."
QPR boss Harry Redknapp

"It was a terrific game, but I'd rather it had been a load of cr*p and we'd won."
Harry reflects after the Hammers were knocked out of the FA Cup by Tottenham

"I had to change the team three times between 10.30am and kick-off. I ended up going into the boot room and finding two kids, Anthony Pulis and Warren Hunt, having a cup of tea. I needed another so I found Shaun Cooper, who was having a meat pie when I told him he was on the bench."

Harry on the task of filling a bench for his injury-hit Portsmouth side

"Mansfield gave us one hell of a game. I feared extra time but we are still on the march, still unbeaten, and I'm still a brilliant manager!"

Pompey's ever-modest manager

"Modric played well. Keane, Defoe and Palacios played well. But I don't want to pick out individuals."

Of course you don't, Harry

"Seriously, the boy glides across the park. If he walked across a puddle, he wouldn't make a splash."

Harry lauds Theo Walcott

"After shooting practice yesterday, I had to drive up the M27 and collect four balls!"

The Portsmouth manager on Benjani's wayward shooting

"From a still picture how does anybody know what Di Canio was doing? He might have been signalling to a teammate about a tactic from a corner. He might have been gesturing a tactical change. He could have been showing that the score was 1-0."

On Paolo Di Canio's one-fingered gesture to Aston Villa fans

"He took a knock on his ankle but we played him some Bob Marley reggae music and he was fine."

Harry on Southampton striker Kenwyne Jones' injury

"It was nothing."

Harry on the training ground clash which saw John Hartson kick Eyal Berkovic in the head

"What he [John Hartson] did was totally out of order."

He considers his earlier view after the public's reaction to it

"Luckily they had a stupid on their side too."

After 10-man Saints hold 10-man Arsenal

"I think they were waiters from Shepherd's Bush."

Spurs boss Harry doesn't rate QPR

"I'll just have a bacon sandwich, a cup of tea and take my dogs out. I've had ups and downs, life is a roller coaster and I try not to get too down or go overboard. It was always going to be nervy. If people thought we were going to smash Milan out of sight, they've not been watching football. We were playing AC Milan, who are top of Serie A and have lost only three games all season, not Raggy-Arsed Rovers."

Harry reflects on Spurs reaching the Champions League quarter-finals

"[Samassi] Abou retaliated but the fellow went down as if he was dead, and then started rolling around."

Harry is not happy

"When I saw the referee put that whistle to his mouth I can't tell you how fantastic that felt for me. It was like winning the pools."

After Portsmouth's vital victory against Middlesbrough

"I thought Nasri might be captain for them, so they would have to shake hands, then we could get them in a room before the game and William could bash him up or something."

The Spurs boss gave the arm band to William Gallas against Arsenal. Samir Nasri refused to shake Gallas' hand because of previous bad blood

"I got the right hump with Gareth [Bale] when their right-back [Bacary Sagna] made a diabolical tackle on him and then Gareth went for a tackle and bumped in and then walked over and shook hands with him. I said, 'What are we? Are we the nice guys or something?'"

Harry on Spurs' comeback to win 3-2 against Arsenal

"It wasn't like Carlos Tevez, who played a few games for West Ham and then wouldn't celebrate for Man City. I had seven years at this club."

On not celebrating Tottenham's goal against Portsmouth in 2009

"How the f*cking hell did he miss that? My missus could have scored that... You keep pussyfooting around with people – what am I supposed to say? Really good try? Really unlucky? He's really done his best with that?"
Darren Bent is not spared after missing an easy chance for Spurs against Portsmouth in 2009

"Van Persie obviously thought, 'Why take the piss out of poor old Southampton? I'll get sent off and make a game of it'."
Harry on the Dutchman's red card for Arsenal against the Saints

"When he picked the ball up, I'd be a liar if I said I thought he would score. I thought he was going to head it."

The Saints boss on Peter Crouch offering to take a penalty

"Lomana LuaLua probably doesn't even know what 4-4-2 is. But when we switched to it, he stuck to his position out wide and he did a great job."

Harry after Portsmouth beat Man United

"I've seen better fights at a wedding."

On a training ground row between Alvin Martin and Matthew Rush

"[Gennaro] Gattuso had a flare-up with Joe Jordan. I don't know why. He obviously hadn't done his homework. He could've picked a fight with somebody else. I know who I'd pick between Joe Jordan and Gennaro Gattuso anyway... Joe all night long. All night long. He's lucky Joe didn't take his teeth out!"

Harry backs Tottenham coach Joe Jordan as the game against AC Milan got heated

"What he might have said, 'F*ck off' to him and that was it. What is he supposed to say? 'Go away old chap, stop nutting me'."

On the headbutt by Gattuso

'ARRY – The funniest Harry Redknapp quotes!

MEDIA CIRCUS

"Am I supposed to come out after and say, 'It was a jolly good decision, I thought he handled it very well'? We shouldn't be being dragged out onto TV three or four minutes after a game. I don't want to go on TV. I'd much rather stay in the dressing room with the players. When I'm asked a question, I give a truthful answer. He [Mark Clattenburg] made a right mess of it all. That would be my answer, and I stand by it 100 per cent. If [the FA] want to make an issue of what I've said, then I'll make some issues as well, don't worry. Don't expect me to come out on TV after a game anymore, ever. I won't do it."

Harry won't speak to the media if the FA charge him for criticising ref Clattenburg over Nani's freak goal against Spurs

"It's a different game when you can buy players and pay them £250,000 a week. To be honest you would have a chance [of winning the Premier League]. I'd fancy you to manage them. You'd win it."

The Tottenham boss to reporters after claiming his net spend was £18m compared to Man City's £190m

"I don't want them going out having Christmas parties. What chance have you got? The press will be waiting, someone will be taking pictures of them. Somebody can just have their eyes closed and it looks like they are boozed. You don't need it."

Harry's a party pooper

"That's it, f*cking interview over! All you're interested in is some f*cking banner!"

Harry, who was back at Portsmouth after a spell at rivals Southampton, refers to a banner unfurled by the fans which said: 'Judas, walk the plank!'. It was Pompey's ninth straight away league defeat

"Oh, I dunno. I've just won a championship last year and just knocked Liverpool out. It's terrible. It's been awful. The chairman should get rid of me."

Harry jokes with reporters after Pompey put Liverpool out of the FA Cup

"You're going to write what you want to write and to f*ck me up on cup final day – I know what's going to happen Rob and you're all barking up the wrong tree. If you say the tax hasn't been declared and it hasn't been paid, I will sue the b*llocks off, yeah everybody at the News of the World, make no mistake, yeah."
Speaking to News of the World reporter Rob Beasley ahead of Tottenham's 2009 League Cup final against Man United

"I'm not allowed to speak to Joe. Are you trying to get me banned by the FA or something?!"
When asked by a reporter if he has spoken directly to Joe Cole about signing for QPR

Reporter: "Harry, what message did you give the players at half-time?"

West Ham's Harry Redknapp: "Just 'play the same as we did first half'. What do you f*cking think I said to them at half-time?"

Reporter: "Dunno."

Redknapp: "'Go and f*cking sit back and let them attack us' or summink? Is that what you think I said? What a f*cking stupid question."

"You weren't allowed to speak to the press when I was playing. If you got caught, you got a fine of a week's wages, which was about £7."

It was different in Harry's day

Redknapp: "We lost [player] with a knee ligament injury and he's having a scan to-day and I'm just hoping it's not as serious as we think it might be. He's not going to be around..."

[A ball hits Redknapp in the back and he turns around].

"Why the f*ck have you kicked that over here? Uh? What? You tried to kick it in the goal and you hit me? Got to get some f*cking brains ain't ya?"

TV interviewer: "Sorry Harry, just a last word on Wolves. It's a big game at Molineux, a big crowd, it's a big match for you."

Redknapp: "Yeah it's a big match... no wonder he's in the f*cking reserves."

'ARRY – The funniest Harry Redknapp quotes!

CALL THE MANAGER

"I've just heard there's a lot of rubbish on Radio 5 that I'm walking out. I'm not leaving. I've got a job to do, especially for these fans. They're the best in the country."

The Portsmouth boss quit for Southampton soon after

"I don't look at my contracts, I don't read one word, I sign at the bottom. Then my accountant rings up and says, 'Harry you've got a £500,000 bonus from the Champions League'."

On picking up bonuses

"Why did I take the job? Skint."

On joining Portsmouth

"I've not done well in this game because I'm a mug."

After guiding Spurs into the Champions League in 2010

"When David Webb was the manager of Bournemouth he never thought training was any good unless there'd been a punch-up."

Harry loves a bit of passion

"You will never get the sack for having an untidy desk. You only get the sack if you lose games and buy bad players."

On how a manager stays employed

"No I haven't resigned, and I've no idea why it is being suggested that I have. This is an outrage, an absolute liberty for people to be putting around this kind of rumour on the internet. It's not true, there's not a chance I will resign. Why should I? I have a year left on my contract."

The Tottenham manager was sacked inside 48 hours

"I am a fantastic football manager not a hard-headed businessman. I've got no business acumen whatsoever."

Harry in court during his tax-evasion trial

"I had promised to manage a side for Tony McCoy for the jockeys' fund which is a great charity but I can't do that now. Funny really, because I was a bit worried about that because I didn't know any of the players – a bit like here really! I was worried how I was going to find a centre half amongst the jockeys with them all being so small. Now I've got a slightly bigger problem."

Harry on taking over relegation-threatened Birmingham

"A big club will always go for that sexy name. I'm not really sexy. You'll have to ask my wife. She'll definitely say 'no'."

Unsexy Harry

"Portsmouth is my club – I feel an immense sense of loyalty and unfulfilled ambition. I could have left but I would have felt a great sense of betrayal. So they're stuck with me now. This will be my last job in football."

The Pompey boss in 2008. He then managed Spurs, QPR, Jordan and Birmingham

"This will definitely be my last club – apart from Swanage maybe. That's close to where I live and it might be nice to finish there!"

The Portsmouth manager doesn't fool us

"Bad results slaughter me, they gut me."

Every defeat hurts

"The Del Boy comparisons piss me off. I'm not like him at all. I've been married 35 years and this is my third football club in 20-odd years. I'm not a ducker and diver. I may be a cockney, but that doesn't mean I fit some silly stereotype."

The Pompey boss sets the record straight

"I always said they will probably end up taking Sir Alex Ferguson out of Old Trafford in a box and I'll probably be exactly the same."

Harry is not planning to retire

"I've got coaching badges but they came out of a Corn Flakes packet."

Harry the coach

"Joe Royle texted me to say keeping us up would be like – was it turning fish into something, or water into wine, or feeding the 5,000? I've never read the Bible but I think he meant it would be a miracle."

After joining QPR in 2012... they ended up relegated

"I threw a plate of sandwiches at Don Hutchison. He sat there, still arguing with me, with cheese and tomato running down his face. You can't do that anymore, especially with all the foreigners. They'd go home."

Harry might now eat the sandwiches

"The days of walking in, shouting and screaming and throwing teacups at players were gone. There is no point effing and blinding at a player who can hardly speak English."

Harry is much calmer these days

"When I was at Bournemouth I kicked a tray of cups up in the air. One hit Luther Blissett on the head. He flicked it on and went all over my suit hanging behind him."

Harry on the striker's skills

"I will never go down the road."

On the chances of leaving Portsmouth for Southampton...

"If I was the invisible man for a day, I'd hang around the QPR dressing room to hear what the players say about me."

Harry on his ideal superpower

"I'm not a wheeler dealer, f*ck off. I'm not a f*cking wheeler and dealer, don't even, don't say that, I'm a f*cking football manager."

The boss puts a TV interviewer right

"You can have all the computers in the world, but your eyes have to be the judge."

On his traditional methods of being a football manager

"If I said I'd go back now I'd be crucified —
that's all I need."

**Harry declares himself out of the running
for the Portsmouth job in 2005... before
going back**

"What are they going to do, shoot me? It's not
war you know."

**He is unfazed about going back to former
club Portsmouth**

"The sad part is that the ones who do well want
to go but you cannot move the ones who are
useless."

Harry on dealing with players

'ARRY – The funniest Harry Redknapp quotes!

REF
JUSTICE

"I'm the last person to ever criticise referees, I never come on TV after games and start moaning about referees. If we get beat, we get beat. I'm not saying we would have won the game or drawn the game, but who knows? We were losing the game at the time 1-0. I still can't understand the decision. It was a complete mess-up, nobody knew what was going on. It was farcical. I think Mark knows he made a mistake, I know that he knows he dealt with it not very well. But it has happened, it's history, let's move on."

Harry blasts Mark Clattenburg after Man United's Nani scored into an empty net, while Spurs keeper Heurelho Gomes was preparing to take a free-kick

"At no time did I use abusive language… The referee came over and told me I was spoiling the fourth official's afternoon by jumping up and down all the time. So I said to him, 'I've got news for you, you're spoiling mine', and that was it."

The Saints boss is sent to the stands after Derby scored a retaken penalty

"At no stage did I ever swear. I just asked the fourth official why the goal was allowed. He said – how you would talk to a six-year-old at school if you were a school teacher – to sit down."

Harry gets a dressing down

"From the start of the game I just felt the referee had no idea whatsoever, it was frightening. Where was he from? Slovakia? Slovenia? I'm sure it's a good league there and he's been handling lots of big games."

Harry fumes at Darko Ceferin after Pompey's 3-0 UEFA Cup defeat away to Braga. The Slovenian disallowed Papa Bouba Diop's header for a foul

"He is supposed to be our best ref, but if he's the best, I'd hate to see the worst."

He's not happy after Howard Webb awarded Man United a penalty against Spurs in 2009

"I accept defeat and have never complained about refereeing decisions in 30 years of managing. Never. But today he got some badly wrong. When he goes home tonight and sees them he'll know he's made a couple of terrible decisions. The linesman, he'll watch it tonight, when his wife's making him a bacon sandwich and he'll think: 'F*ck me what have I done there today?'"

On ref Chris Foy missing a Ryan Shawcross hand ball which stopped Younes Kaboul's goal-bound effort for Tottenham

'ARRY – The funniest Harry Redknapp quotes!

LIFESTYLE CHOICE

"I'm not really one for being careful about every word I say. If you're going to sit down and keep talking a load of cobblers, what's the point?"

Never one to skirt around the issue

"I know the odd indulgence doesn't hurt players from time to time... besides, what can you do? Can you follow a player home to check if his missus is giving him steak and kidney pie for tea instead of pasta?"

On players' diets

"I'm a compulsive bird feeder. I hate to think of them going hungry. Bit mad, innit?"

The bird man

LIFESTYLE CHOICE

"There was an Italian restaurant in town called Di Luca's and the owner told our keeper if he kept a clean sheet he would give him free pizzas for life. We beat them [Man United] 2-0 and for a while he was getting free pizzas. I bought that restaurant and stopped the free pizza. I said, 'Sorry Ian, under new management'."

Harry ended free pizza for keeper Ian Leigh after Bournemouth shocked United in 1984

"When you're a millionaire, winning a few quid on a horse means nothing."

Harry on the Pompey players' disinterest in racing

"He is a brilliant man, an unbelievable character. For the cup final, I took them out before and we all went to an Italian restaurant. Hermann got on the karaoke and brought out the best Elvis Presley suit, the white one with the big shoulders. Hermann's voice is diabolical, but the actions are fantastic."

The Spurs manager on his former player, Portsmouth defender Hermann Hreidarsson

"I don't think he's a boy to go abroad. The first chance he gets, he goes back to his family in Wales."

Harry on Gareth Bale in 2012. Months later, he joins Real Madrid

LIFESTYLE CHOICE

"I write like a two-year-old and I can't spell...
I can't work a computer, I don't know what an
email is, I can't, I have never sent a fax and I've
never even sent a text message. I have a big
problem, I can't write so I don't keep anything.
I am the most disorganised person, I am
ashamed to say, in the world...you talk to
anybody at the football club. I don't write. I
couldn't even fill a team sheet in."

On literacy and technology

"With the foreign players it's more difficult. Most
of them don't even bother with the golf, they
don't want to go racing. They don't even drink."

Harry on a different breed of footballer

"Hopefully he [Malky Mackay] will learn from what he has done but everyone does the tweeting and texting. I don't send text messages, but I do receive them with sick jokes. I don't read them, they make me ill."

Harry's not much of a texter

"I love animals so much, all animals. Apart from cats, I'm a little bit scared of cats."

He stays away from felines

"There's no problem with people having the occasional drink, but if you have to get drunk, you shouldn't be drinking."

Harry makes his point

LIFESTYLE CHOICE

"I got some sweets and the next thing I felt someone pull my overcoat. There are two guys on their knees in front of me and they've got my trousers and they keep pulling them. I'm pushing them away but while I'm doing that they're rifling my pockets."

On getting mugged while in Madrid

"I just probably looked stupid or something, and they thought, 'Here's one here, he's not Spanish, we're looking for a foreigner'."

Harry explains why he thought he was targeted by the Spanish muggers

"We've got sports scientists who insist it's important for the lads to eat after games to refuel, even if it's 2am. I used to refuel after games at West Ham until half past three in the morning in a different way – but then I'm old school."

Harry on the good ol' days

"I haven't seen my missus, Sandra, all week. She might be delighted, I am not."

Like many managers, he is a workaholic

"I still don't like calling her a dog, she was so much better than that."

Harry reminisces about his dog Rosie

"Was I scared of going to prison? Yes I was. You're relying on 12 people who might not like you. They might have been Arsenal fans for all I knew. One had a stained jacket, for goodness sake."

On his 2013 court case

"That's part of the territory. I wouldn't go out and get drunk and start falling around or pulling some old slag tomorrow night, would I? I'm not that stupid. Because somebody will catch you out. Having said that, Tiger Woods didn't do too bad."

Harry won't be going clubbing

"I'll implement a strong rule next season that drinking is a no-no here. Footballers should dedicate their lives to playing. Footballers should not drink. You shouldn't put diesel in a Ferrari. I know it's hard but they are earning big money, they are role models to kids."

Harry reacts after Ledley King was arrested outside a London nightclub

"I feed foxes, I'm not supposed to, but I love it. The squirrels get a lot – I bought the plastic containers, they chewed the bottom and the nuts fell out, so I had to buy the steel ones. They work better."

Harry the feeder

Journalist: "Have you received any death threats?"

Harry Redknapp: "Only from the wife when I didn't do the washing up!"

Southampton's Harry Redknapp ahead of the Portsmouth clash

"You find yourself being questioned by a man who is probably 100 times better educated that I am. He's a clever man. He's probably gone to Eton. I'm standing there uneducated really and I have to try to stand your corner."

On being prosecuted in 2012

"We were all on the coach waiting to go to Stockport and [Florin] Raducioiu was in Harvey Nichols shopping with his missus."

The West Ham manager is shocked

"You think I put my hand on the bible and told lies? That's an insult, Mr Black, that's an insult."

Harry on honesty in court

"Don't be fooled by the way I look. People say you eventually start to grow to look like the missus but I wouldn't be that unkind to my Sandra."

Harry the charmer

"If you can't pass the ball properly, a bowl of pasta's not going to make that much difference!"
Harry, when asked if a change of diet had contributed to Spurs' 4-4 draw at Arsenal

"When I heard the draw I was out on the golf course. I had an eight-iron in one hand and my mobile in the other. When we came out with United, my club went further than the ball."
The Pompey boss on the FA Cup draw

"They're busy cows! I don't like it. I've got no time for it at all."
Harry on WAGs

"We went to watch a show - Billy Joel. Half of the foreign lads weren't quite sure who Billy Joel was, but I enjoyed it anyway. For the Charlton game I'll really punish them - I'll take them to see Mamma Mia."

The Portsmouth manager celebrates a 3-1 win over Fulham

"There is nothing like the buzz of winning on a Saturday, but there is nothing like the low of losing either. I had so much trouble sleeping that for a while I was addicted to Night Nurse. When I told Sandra she thought I was talking about some bird in suspenders."

Harry gets a bit fruity

"QPR is my team now. The grandkids are all getting QPR kit this week."

Harry forcing Christmas presents on his family members

"I'd rather give you a hundred grand than nick a few quid off you. We're givers not takers."

Harry during his 2012 court case

"They searched the house and took a computer away that I bought my wife two years ago – I think she learnt to turn it on four weeks ago."

The Pompey boss after police raided his home during a 'football corruption' probe

"I had three pie and mash. I nicked an extra one. I think some of the foreign lads weren't too sure, but we ate their portions."

Harry remembers when David Beckham took the Spurs squad out for pie and mash

"It was only one picture and it's only Ledley who looks like he has fallen asleep."

He plays down photos of his Tottenham players appearing tipsy during a night out

"My only chance is if he has a heavy one in the bar and I have an early one."

On the challenge of beating former England cricketer Andrew Flintoff at golf

LIFESTYLE CHOICE

"I don't think that's going to do Peter any good."
On reports that striker Peter Crouch's girlfriend Abby Clancy wants to kill the Spurs manager for selling Crouch to Stoke

"I'm sure Stoke is a beautiful place... I know Tony [Pulis] don't live there."
Harry on the positives of living in Stoke

"Do you think Paolo Maldini at 41 is going out on a Saturday night and drinking with lager coming out of his ears and falling over? I don't see it somehow."
On English football's love of a pint

'ARRY – The funniest Harry Redknapp quotes!

CAN YOU MANAGE?

"The only trouble is that he's admitted he wants to be a porn star. Maybe I can get another year out of him before he decides to do that."

Harry is thwarted at trying to sign Benoit Assou-Ekotto for Birmingham

"I took Kanu on the Tuesday before the first game of the season because I never had any strikers. He said he hadn't kicked a ball since last season and I asked him if he'd been training. He said 'Yes, I've been running around the park some days' and I thought 'Yeah, I bet you have!'"

The Portsmouth boss on Kanu

CAN YOU MANAGE?

"The world is full of nutters who are going to send you messages slagging you off."

Harry after QPR's Chris Samba received Twitter abuse following his display against Fulham

"They keep coming up with these people – someone sitting up there eating a big hamburger with holes in his jeans."

On the Pompey owner changes

"Barcelona want him? Maybe we'll do a straight swap with Messi."

The QPR boss is happy to let go of Adel Taarabt

"I took him to my house and he heard the dogs barking. 'Dogs! I no like dogs,' he said and he froze. 'They're not dogs, Amdy,' I assured him. 'They're bulldogs. They're more vicious than dogs. Half-dog, half-bull. If you try to escape, they bite your balls off'. We made sure he knew that the dogs were left downstairs at night. The next day he signed for £1.5million."

On signing Amdy Faye for Pompey

"It is still the best time Portsmouth has had since Nelson left."

The Portsmouth boss hopes to head off to Europe like Lord Nelson

CAN YOU MANAGE?

"We'll train Christmas Day. I don't give a sh*t about Christmas. I'm going to be the most miserable person you have ever seen in your whole life."

After Pompey's 3-0 loss at Southampton

"He's Australian. He's in the Commonwealth. They fought the war with us. I know that might sound like b*llocks to you but we let foreign people in who have no allegiance to this country."

Harry is upset over the delay of Hayden Foxe's work permit

"At Bournemouth, Shaun Teale's missus nearly ran me over after a row over about one hundred quid. She marched down to the training ground over some minor contractual issue, gave me a mouthful, I told her to p*ss off, and the next thing I knew she was reversing out of the car park so fast she nearly took me with her."

The manager is nearly mowed down by Shaun Teale's wife

"I should get out now – I've taken this team as far as I can."

Harry after guiding new club Spurs to five wins out of six

"These agents get you over to see this fantastic striker you can take on loan. You get there and he's on the bench. On Friday I'm stood outside a hotel in Alaves at 4 o'clock in the morning, pissing down with rain… I thought to myself 'I wonder if Arsene Wenger or Alex Ferguson would be stood outside this hotel at 4am in Alaves? What am I doing?'"

On the pains of scouting players

"If I had said we were going to finish fifth in the Premier League a couple of years ago, you would all have thought I would end up in the nuthouse, wouldn't you?"

Harry on Portsmouth's stellar season

"Two [substitutes] were asleep with hats pulled down and blankets over them. I said, 'I'm sorry to drag you up here, I know it's cold and you could be home with the missus with a cup of tea. It's hard for 30 grand a week to watch the game."

Harry's sarcastic take on the modern-day substitute

"Where are we in relation to Europe? Not too far from Dover."

He plays down West Ham's chances of qualifying for Europe in 1999

"I don't get involved in transfers in any way, shape or form."

Harry after Portsmouth chief Milan Mandaric said he was a 'wheeler dealer'

"We're down to the bare bones."

The manager's common phrase, citing injury problems in his squad, when looking to acquire new players

"I've just been given a video recording of the game and I'm going to tape Neighbours over it."

He can't bare to watch West Ham's goalless draw with Southampton

"There's a Burton's 10 minutes from where we live. She probably thought it was there."

Harry on reports he didn't get the England job because his wife didn't want to live near St George's Park National Football Centre, in Burton-upon-Trent

"If you pay them the wages they'll come. We all kid ourselves: 'I've wanted to play for Tottenham since I was two, I had pictures of Jimmy Greaves on my wall'. It's a load of bull. Here's £80,000 a week. Lovely jubbly."

Ever the cynic

CAN YOU MANAGE?

"To me, there's no point in having confrontation for the sake of it. Look at Ruud Gullit. Can you tell me that he was a shrewd manager in what he did to Rob Lee, who was captain of Newcastle and Alan Shearer's best mate? Why make problems for yourself?"

Harry blasts Ruud Gullit's treatment of Rob Lee and Alan Shearer at Newcastle. Gullit forced Lee to train alone and dropped Shearer for the big derby with Sunderland

"You can't get f*ck-all for a million nowadays."

Harry refers to the £1m he paid for Hammers flop Marco Boogers

"If you asked me if I wanted to sell my car and I said 'no', that is the end of it. You don't keep ringing me up."

Harry hits out at Sunderland for their never-ending pursuit of Darren Bent

"Before I signed Luther Blissett for Bournemouth, my chairman at the time said, 'Harry, they tell me he's over the hill. Why are we signing him?' I said, 'He'll score goals'. In his first game he scored four against Hull. After the game the chairman said, 'We haven't seen the best of him yet'. I said, 'I think we have'."

On Luther Blissett's goal-scoring pedigree

CAN YOU MANAGE?

"We've won seven out the last eight league games, and we can't do any more than that."

Maybe win eight?

"They can offer him free chicken for life and we can't compete with that."

He says Blackburn have a better chance of signing David Beckham than Spurs

"He won't talk to me on Twitter, as I don't know what Twitter is."

Harry on QPR transfer target Peter Odemwingie

"I'll be mightily relieved when this transfer window closes. Morning, noon and night over the past few weeks it has been non-stop phone calls. I took the missus out for a meal. I was outside the restaurant for a good hour-and-a-half negotiating with three other parties."

Harry on wheeler-dealing

"I told my players Frank Lampard has got 17 goals from midfield this season, but they just said, 'Perhaps that's why he's on 150 grand a week'."

Harry tries to motivate the Pompey players

"I was in bed with my wife last night – if you're as ugly as me you want to talk about football. And she said, 'Harry, if you're drawing, push Trevor Sinclair up front'. So I gambled and it worked."

The West Ham boss gets tactical advice

"I hear that all the time that if [the players] get relegated they want to go because they don't want to play in the Championship, but if they f*cking played better, then they would not be in the Championship so that's a load of cobblers."

Harry on QPR's battle against the drop in 2013

"I left a couple of my foreigners out last week and they started talking in 'foreign'. I knew what they were saying: 'Blah, blah, blah, le b*stard manager, f*cking useless b*stard!'"

The interpreter

"We're playing our usual away formation. A bloke up front who can't run and two wide men who don't track back."

Harry in sarcastic mood

"Someone has rung up and tried to put £50 on me because they've heard some silly rumour. It's free publicity for William Hill."

On reports he is leaving Tottenham

CAN YOU MANAGE?

"To be in the top four alongside teams like Chelsea, Manchester United, Liverpool and Arsenal is incredible."

The Portsmouth manager after their draw with Arsenal. That's five Harry

"I woke up Thursday to read I am on the brink of losing my job and going down the pan. I thought I had this dream I had just beaten Manchester United and won Manager of the Month. It must have been someone else."

On reports he is facing the sack at Portsmouth

"I thought I was David Pleat as I was running up the touchline to celebrate – except I haven't got his colour shoes."

Harry on recreating the Pleat jig

"We're clearly a top-six side, even though the league doesn't lie."

On West Ham stuck at the bottom of the table after six matches

"If you ask me, I'll take penalties. We've been practising."

On Spurs coming back from a 4-0 first-leg Champions League defeat against Real Madrid

CAN YOU MANAGE?

"It's like being on the Titanic and seeing there is only one lifeboat left and we are all trying to dive into it!"

The Southampton boss on being the team that finishes above the relegation zone

"I tape over most of them with Corrie or Neighbours. Most of them are crap. They can f*cking make anyone look good. I signed Marco Boogers off a video. He was a good player but a nutter. They didn't show that on the video."

On the danger of signing players from video tapes

"I don't know this guy Velimir Zajec and I never will know him. He will never know me. Never. No chance. It won't happen."

Harry on news that a director of football is being appointed at Pompey

"The Arsenal fans hate Adebayor so I am sure that will make the Tottenham fans like him."

On bringing Emmanuel Adebayor to Spurs

"This is the final straw. You'd have to be a certifiable lunatic to want to work with that lot."

Harry is fed up with the players

CAN YOU MANAGE?

"I was offered him about four years ago when he was only 19. I remember watching him play in a game against Barnet reserves – he looked decent enough but this was just after I had all those problems with the Romanian lads and I thought the last thing I needed was a Ukrainian."

On turning down the chance to buy Andriy Shevchenko

"I've learned my lesson with the foreigners. I won't be buying any more of them in the near future."

Harry shortly before signing Titi Camara and Rigobert Song in 2000

"Harry was overruled. The club did not want some nutter having a go."

The Saints boss on having a bodyguard for his safety against Portsmouth in 2005

"When they got £5m compensation for me, they were really happy to accept the money. In fact, I think they called a taxi for me."

Harry on departing Pompey for Tottenham in 2008

"I've got a sh*t weekend coming up, so has my family and everybody else who comes near me."

After Spurs' loss at Bolton in 2009

"I bought a player and within two weeks he doesn't want to be in England. He doesn't like the way we play and he doesn't like to be tackled in training."

Harry on the risk in signing foreign stars

"As for wages, the players have had a trim, the chairman has had a trim and I have had a short back and sides."

On Southampton's cutbacks after they were relegated from the top flight

"I won't slit my throat over it."

He is not getting down after being sacked by Spurs

"I was going to fly out and scout them tomorrow, but they're playing Atletico Madrid, and the last time I watched them I got robbed!"

Harry is reluctant to watch Real Madrid

"She lifted it and I felt my back go and I had sciatica for the next three nights, so I went missing when they were doing it yesterday."

Harry manages to avoid the Spurs yoga class

"I'll give him Thursdays off, maybe he's busy on Thursday nights."

He has a dig at Jermain Defoe for wanting to avoid Europa League matches

CAN YOU MANAGE?

"We could do with Gary, see if he is available to do a bit up front for us."

Harry reckons Gary Lineker could get a place in his Spurs team

"It's not the Yorkshire Ripper I'm signing, is it?"

He doesn't feel William Gallas has a bad rep

"He can't do too much. I don't know if he can even swim."

Harry on Ledley King's troublesome knees

"He got cramp everywhere – even his ears!"

On Steven Caulker's availability

'ARRY – The funniest Harry Redknapp quotes!

A FUNNY OLD GAME

"Where they find some owners now, I don't know. I remember the first guy they brought in at Portsmouth from Saudi Arabia somewhere. He looked like they pulled him off the stall outside. He looked like the only Arab who didn't have oil in his garden."

Harry's unique take on foreign ownership

"I don't really want to see the owners have their pants taken down like they have in the past."

Harry reckons the QPR wage bill is too high

"Judging by the shape of his face, he must have headed a lot of goals."

Harry on Iain Dowie

A FUNNY OLD GAME

"Even when they had Moore, Hurst and Peters, West Ham's average finish was about 17th. It just shows how useless the other eight of us were."

Looking back on his days as a player

"[Stan] Collymore should have played for England [against Sweden] last week, I mean he is good at beating a Swede."

It's a low blow from Harry

"The manager's a young lad who I've heard good things about. Charlie McFarland, he's a good coach...."

On Notts County's manager... Ian McParland

"The reception I got at Upton Park wasn't too bad considering I now manage one of their biggest rivals. Mind you, it helped that I didn't get out of my seat for 90 minutes."

The Spurs boss on returning to the Hammers

"Stuart can kiss goodbye to a knighthood but credit for being brave."

Harry on Team GB boss Stuart Pearce not selecting David Beckham for the Olympics

"Let them have it, good luck to them."

On Manchester United and Manchester City's Europa League chances

A FUNNY OLD GAME

"Running tracks and football grounds sit together about as well as putting a swimming pool on Centre Court."

Commenting on stadiums that can host both football and athletics

"It was as if he was a professor of chess sitting there as if he was studying every move while these other idiots are shouting and screaming."

On Arsene Wenger's arrival in England

"Billy Big Head – what's he doing today? Where's he been? What's he up to?"

Harry is thankful he doesn't have to manage Mario Balotelli at Spurs

"Football supporters don't care what you do as long as you're a good footballer. They would sing Saddam Hussein's name if he scored a few goals for their team."

QPR's Harry Redknapp on fickle fans

"I held a meeting with my players. I told them about the agent and that allegedly he had paid some of his fee to the player. All of them wanted his phone number because they had never heard of an agent who wanted to give a player any money!"

Classic Redknapp humour from his time at Portsmouth

"We signed Milko Millman. We thought he was foreign as he came from Jersey. There was another reason behind the deal. At the time, you couldn't get tomatoes anywhere – he turned up with a whole box for the manager."

Harry on playing for Bournemouth during the 70s

"The Premiership is going to be tougher than ever next season and if you stand still you end up going backwards."

Science was never the best subject for Pompey's Harry

"It's a nonsense. If that's the best they could get out of three hours of sitting with me and trying to stitch me up, it's sad. The worst part is that when the bill came up, the other four scumbags got up and left me with the bill."

Harry fumes at being left with the bill after meeting with undercover newspaper reporters probing football corruption

"I told my chairman that David O'Leary paid £18m for Rio Ferdinand and Leeds have given him £5m in share options. I bring in £18m and all I get is a bacon sandwich."

Harry feels he should be better rewarded

"Why shouldn't he go down there? He's not committed a murder, has he?"

Southampton manager Harry Redknapp on ex-Saints boss Gordon Strachan going for the Portsmouth vacancy

"I wouldn't trust the FA to show me a good manager if their lives depended on it."

QPR's Harry is not a fan

"I laugh when I hear stories, 'Wolves have got relegated, people are going to come in and take all their players'. If they were so good they wouldn't have got relegated."

The Tottenham boss says it how it is

"The Germans were better than us. Then, at 4-1, we needed a goal and we took off [Jermain] Defoe and sent on [Emile] Heskey!"

Harry takes a swipe at England manager Fabio Capello after the defeat to Germany in the 2010 World Cup

"Everyone had a rattle and they went just to enjoy the game. If that sounds a rose-tinted or nostalgic memory, I'm sorry, but it's true. Then, for me, and my dad, it was a cheese roll at a little cafe up the road, the 106 bus and then the 227 back to Poplar."

On watching West Ham as a fan

"It's almost certainly too late for him to make it into England's Euro 2016 squad but I do not think he would let anyone down if given the chance."

He rates 25-cap Jamaica international Wes Morgan

"Bob's got it all now. The old South Bank named after him at Upton Park, statues outside the ground and at Wembley Stadium. They even use his name to sell West Ham United merchandise these days. When he was alive they didn't want to know him. I saw him get slung out of there for not having a ticket."

Harry on Bobby Moore's legacy

"If people are stupid enough to shout abuse, then they need their heads looking at."

Harry on coming back to Portsmouth as Tottenham's manager

"I shall not be interfering with Graham Rix."

On his relationship as Portsmouth's director of football with the club's manager

"He's disappeared to Azerbaijan, or somewhere ridiculous in the world."

Harry on Tony Adams

"Daniel Levy was behind the deal that took Michael Carrick to Tottenham. It certainly wasn't that French manager, Jacques Santini. He didn't know Michael Carrick from Michael Jackson."

The manager doesn't particularly admire Santini's transfer knowledge

"Everyone f*cking jumps all over you. They don't care Michael Carrick's just 19. When he gave the ball away the other week there was 20,000 people c*nting him off. He give a bad ball and they are all f*cking 'weeerrrr'."

On the West Ham supporters

"England can sometimes be quite painful to watch, and I know from some of the [Tottenham] players that it is not an enjoyable experience for them, either."

He's as honest as ever

"First of all I had to find the bloody cabinet. When I eventually did, I opened the doors and out flew two bats, three Japanese soldiers and Lord Lucan!"

On West Ham's trophy cabinet

"When I heard the news I thought it was April 1st."

On Sven-Goran Eriksson joining Notts County

"I didn't know anything about it, I swear. Nor did Dave Bassett. We were sitting there saying 'What's happening here?'. It is frightening. A nightmare."

He cannot understand the new offside law

"Jimmy Greaves would walk past four defenders, send the goalie one way, roll the ball into the opposite corner and walk away as if to say, 'What am I here for?' Then have a fag at half-time."

Harry on the legendary Tottenham striker

"Jamie would meet my dad after the game and take him back to the station with Steve McManaman. Dad said to me, 'I felt bad, as I had a roll for Jamie, but not Steve'. I said, 'A roll? He's getting 30 grand a week'. Every week after that he took two rolls."

Harry on his father feeding son Jamie at Liverpool

"A mate said to me after watching Messi destroy a team on his own that the Argentine looks like the sort of bloke you'd find sitting in a bookies in the afternoon, smoking a fag and betting on horses."

On Lionel Messi's appearance

"It's like the X Factor. You're either good or you're not. It's not a case of going back, meeting up with the judges for a couple of days, having a chat and saying, 'You should be voting for me really. I'm a sexy bird, I'll get my gear off for you'."

On England's failed bid for the 2018 World Cup

"He used to watch the game like a professor when all the other nutters were jumping up and down, shouting and screaming. Now, he's joined the nutters. In fact, he's one of the key nutters."

The Spurs boss on Arsene Wenger

"We'd run up the Epping Road, cars and lorries flying by, then it was walk and run for two hours. Bobby Moore was always at the back doing it in his own time, while Brian Dear would hitch a lift on a milk float."

On pre-season training as a West Ham player in the 60s

"I don't like these silly phone-in programmes. People come on who don't know what the hell they are talking about and say things like, 'Sack the manager because the team played crap today'."

Harry sticks up for sacked Spurs manager Martin Jol

"We should be able to produce someone who can manage England, and let's be honest, they can't do any worse than what they [Eriksson and Capello] have done."

Harry on England managers

"You have got people saying stuff behind you with little kids shouting filth. I don't bring my kids up to talk like that."

After getting abuse from Aston Villa fans

"The only relaxed boss is Big Ron. He had me drinking pink champagne – before the match."

Harry on Ron Atkinson

'ARRY – The funniest Harry Redknapp quotes!

PLAYER POWER

"I remember meeting Vinny Samways for the first time at a Bobby Charlton coaching school I did about 30 years ago. He was nine at the time, and I remember after that, dropping him home a few times because his dad was doing 25 years for armed robbery!"

Harry remembers the young midfielder

"My missus fancies him. Even I don't know whether to play him or f*ck him."

The West Ham boss on midfielder Dani

"Samassi Abou don't speak the English too good."

A bit of irony from the Hammers manager

"This man was on another planet. He went to Barnsley one night and I've never seen a performance like it. When I took him off with four minutes left, 14,000 people stood up, clapping him. He was that good. Good players can play anywhere. If they can't play at Barnsley then they're not top players."

On working with Robert Prosinecki at Portsmouth

"He played in a reserve team game the other day, and I could have run about more than he did."

Harry criticises his QPR midfielder Adel Taarabt after defeat to Liverpool

"I just told [the translator] to tell [Pavlyuchenko] to f*cking run around a bit. The boy himself just kept nodding his head. He might be thinking inside, 'What's this t*sser saying to me?'"

Harry's reaction after Roman Pavlyuchenko got the Spurs winner against Liverpool

"He drove me mad in training. Technically, he was outstanding but he always seemed to be playing with his hair."

Referring to former midfielder Gareth Bale

"There's no doubt Bentley has balls – and plenty of 'em."

Harry on David Bentley

"I can't keep protecting people, who don't want to run about and train, and are about three stone overweight. What am I supposed to keep saying? Keep getting your 60, 70 grand a week and don't train? What's the game coming to?"
QPR's manager on Adel Taarabt's lack of fitness

"He can't help being good-looking – he was born like it, I suppose."
Harry fancies Glen Johnson

"He's cocky and arrogant but show him a goal and he's away, like a wind-up toy."
His assessment of striker Jermain Defoe

"The only reason he has lost weight is because he has had tonsillitis, that's the only way we could get any weight off of him. He is not fit to play a game, that's the truth. He is the worst professional I have ever come across and I have been his only ally at QPR for the past three years."

Harry after Taarabt had slimmed down

"He is an absolute freak."

On Ledley King's ability to keep playing despite his knee trouble

"He's had a couple of dickie moments..."

Harry is diplomatic about Heurelho Gomes

"I've got to be honest, you wouldn't want to have a fight with this fella. He's a big 'un…. I think we better give him an extra year on his contract in case he 'cops the needle with me."

On new QPR signing Oguchi Onyewu

Journalist: "What's happening about Marco Negri, Harry?"

Harry: "Negri? Don't know what you are talking about? Who's he?"

Journalist: "That bloke from Rangers running around the training ground behind you."

Harry: "Oh that Negri. Yeah we are having a look at him."

Redknapp fails to fool a reporter

"One reason he's improved so much is he's stopped messing about with his barnet."

Harry on Gareth Bale's hair

"I used to make sure I put him on a team in training where nobody would kick him, because otherwise it would all blow up. He was volatile. He'd kick one wide and I'd used to say it was a goal. It's Paolo. Got to keep him sweet for Saturday."

Harry on buttering up Paolo Di Canio

"He was happy, apart from when I called him John Utaka. Other than that he was fine."

Referring to Tottenham's Jonathan Obika

"The most common thing I'd get from Kanu was a message every Monday morning with the exact same message, that at some points it felt pre-recorded. 'Boss, the King cannot come into training. I have an upset stomach'."

On working with Nwankwo Kanu

"Not speaking English is a problem. You've always got his interpreter running around the training ground. Sometimes you pass the ball through the middle and he chases it. And the interpreter is running alongside him and he gets in there and heads it into the net."

Training-ground games with Russian striker Roman Pavlyuchenko

"No, I haven't sent him the bill. I just hope he's happy at his new club."

Harry after David Bentley soaked his suit with water following Spurs' qualification for the Champions League in 2010

"He came to me and said, 'Futre 10'. I said, 'Eusebio, Pele, Maradona 10 – no, f*cking 16'. We argued. He threw the shirt down, trod on it and left."

Harry on West Ham's Paulo Futre

"John Hartson's got more previous than Jack the Ripper."

On the striker's disciplinary record

"He's a smashing professional and a leader. He's like Bobby Moore in that respect, though he wouldn't have made it into Bobby's drinking school."

Harry on Paolo Di Canio

"The older players all love him. When we took him to Newcastle before he broke into the side, they all started singing his name as he boarded the coach."

On West Ham's Joe Cole

"Kanu? He's about 47."

When asked the age of Portsmouth's Kanu, who claims to be 31

"The lad went home to the Ivory Coast and got a bit of food poisoning. He must have eaten a dodgy missionary or something."

Harry on Samassi Abou's unknown illness

"Bloody hell, Ade, you are on 200 grand a week and you can't afford to pay a £50 fine."

On the tight Emmanuel Adebayor

"I gave him a bollocking. And now I feel bad. I said to him in the dressing room, 'Benji, you've been a silly boy'. He probably won't eat his fish and chips now, will he?"

The Pompey boss on Benjani who missed a late penalty

"He looks like Socrates. He runs like him. If he can play like him we'll be all right."

Harry compares Sandro to the Brazil legend – and not the Greek philosopher

"I helped him a bit with his crosses today. He needs to get his foot around the ball a bit. If he can do that, I think he has a future in the game."

Harry gives advice to David Beckham who was training with Tottenham

"He is a bit of a fruitcake but he's got amazing ability."

QPR boss Harry on Adel Taarabt

'ARRY – The funniest Harry Redknapp quotes!

SCARY

"I never walk in after games and complain about a referee but this guy is scary. He's a poor referee and I've seen him make a mess of so many games. He's really not good enough."

Harry reacts to referee Steve Tanner's display in Tottenham's 2-0 defeat against West Brom

"I admit the future for England looks a bit scary to me. No one should kid themselves England are overloaded with fantastic talent coming through. They're not."

Harry comments on England's terrible 2010 World Cup

"It don't seem 10 minutes ago. That's what's scary. But I must have been doing something right, mustn't I?"

The boss reflects on his long career in the game in a 2008 interview

"What he can achieve is scary. He has everything – he's six feet, can head it, has a great left foot and great touch."

Harry on 'scary' Gareth Bale

"It would have scared me to death to have sold him."

He is frightened again by Bale

"If I think too much about next season, I will be scared stiff again."

On taking Portsmouth up to the Premier League in 2003

"To be fair, when you looked at our run-in, it was almost scary."

Harry on Tottenham's 'horrifying' fixture list at the end of 2009/10

"It's scary that they cannot find someone who cares and has the money to back the club up."

He reflects on Pompey's financial troubles

SCARY

"This is a football club that has been put together by I don't know who, and I don't know how. It's a mishmash of players with people playing where they want to play. It's scary."

Harry while managing Spurs in 2009

"Harry is very similar to [Slaven] Bilic, but is scarier in the dressing room if we're losing at half-time."

Luka Modric finds this word "scary" is catching!

'ARRY – The funniest Harry Redknapp quotes!

Printed in Poland
by Amazon Fulfillment
Poland Sp. z o.o., Wrocław